HILARIOUS DANCE, CHEER, AND GYMNASTICS
JOKES AND PUNS

Text by Megan Woodward

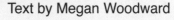

STONE ARCH BOOKS
a capstone imprint

Published by Stone Arch Books, an imprint of Capstone.
1710 Roe Crest Drive
North Mankato, Minnesota 56003
capstonepub.com

Library of Congress Cataloging-in-Publication Data
is available on the Library of Congress website.
ISBN: 9781669074885 (library binding)
ISBN: 9781669075042 (paperback)
ISBN: 9781669075158 (ebook PDF)

ummary: If you love to dance, cheer, or do gymnastics—
and love to laugh—then this book is for you! With more
than 200 hysterical jokes, riddles, and puns, you and
your friends will be laughing for hours!

Editor: Aaron Sautter
Designer: Jaime Willems
Production: Whitney Schaefer
Design Elements: Nana Chen,
Shutterstock/Vector FX

Printed and bound in China. PO 5827

TABLE OF CONTENTS

What is a cat's favorite ballet step?

Paw-de-Purr-ay!

What did the ballet dancer do when he was wrongfully accused?

Entered a not-guilty *plié*.

What ballet step is best done with a friend?

A *Peer*-ouette.

Knock Knock.
Who's there?

It's Pa, duh!
It's Pa duh, who?

No, it's *pas de deux*.

Did you know there's a new ballet called the *Buttcracker*.

It's a work of fart!

Why do ballerinas like surprises?

It keeps them on their toes.

What is a ballet dancer's favorite soup?

Ara-*bisque*.

What do you call a dancing sheep?

A *Baaa*-lerina.

Why were the ballet dancers melting cheese?

To practice their *fondus*.

What do you call a ballerina who likes to dish out insults?

Diss-graceful.

Why did the ballet dancer invite so many people to his party?

He wanted a good *turnout*.

How do you spot a wealthy ballerina?

She has a private *jeté*.

What ballet do lazy dancers perform?

The Nut-*slacker*.

Why do ballerinas wear their hair in buns?

Taco shells are too messy.

What did the ballet dancer say when accused of breaking the law?

"I am well within my tights."

Why was the ballerina sent out of class?

For having a poor *attitude*.

Why did the ballerina win the argument?

She had a good *pointe*.

Why did the ballet dancer let his beard grow?

He wanted to do contempor-*hairy* style!

What is a ballet dancer's favorite dessert?

Swan cake!

How do ballet dancers remember things?

They make a *tendu* list.

Why did the ballerinas show up in number 22 jerseys?

They were told to wear tu-tus.

What is a squirrel's favorite ballet?

The Nutcracker.

What ballet step is out of style?

Passé.

What advice did Yoda give the ballet dancer?

"*Tendu* or not *tendu*. There is no try."

What is a ghost's favorite ballet step?

Scare-abesque!

Why didn't the ballerina show up to class?

She was on *relevé*-cation!

HIP HOP HIJINKS

What's a bunny's favorite style of dance?

Hip hop!

Why do hip hop dancers get louder at bedtime?

They like to pump up their jammies!

Why did the Easter Bunny go to hip hop class?

It was great *eggs*-ercise!

What do car trunks and hip hop dancers have in common?

They can both pop and lock.

Why did the hip hop dancer send back her salad?

The beet was off.

One hip hop dancer passed another on the street. He said, "Hey, why are you walking, man?"

The other dancer said, "Because I'm tired of doing the Running Man!"

A police officer pulled over a car that kept stopping suddenly.

"Sorry officer," said the driver, "I was just brake-dancing."

Why is breakdancing so confusing?

It really makes your head spin.

Why do breakdancers love flowers?

They're Bee-boys.

What do you get when a cow starts breakdancing?

A lot of power *moos!*

What do you call a bull dancing in a china shop?

A break dancer!

BALLROOM BANTER

Where do ballroom dancers sleep?

In the bed-*rhumba*.

What has four legs but does the two-step?

Ballroom dance partners.

What's the best dance to do at a playground?

The Swing.

I tripped during ballroom class.

Now I'm all tangoed up!

Who taught Micky Mouse how to ballroom dance?

Waltz Disney.

Sometimes you have to step on people's toes to be successful.

Unless you're a ballroom dancer.

What did the dancer tell herself when she was feeling discouraged?

I think I can-can.

Why did the ballroom dancer buy a robot vacuum?

He wanted to learn the rhumba.

What salsa dance is a sheep good at?

The *baaaa*-chata.

What happens when ballroom dancers have too much sugar?

They start bouncing off the *waltz*.

What's a ballroom dancer's favorite hot sauce?

Srira-cha cha cha!

I took some salsa classes.

Now I'm a master at dips!

What is a salsa dancer's favorite dessert?

Lemon *merengé* pie.

What do you call a salsa-dancing ape?

An orangu-tango!

What kind of dance goes best with chips?

The salsa.

What do you call a pink bird with great rhythm?

A flamingo dancer.

What is a ballroom dancer's favorite insect?

The jitterbug.

What is a mother's favorite dance?

The *Mom*-bo!

Why did the ballroom dancer have trouble brushing her hair?

It was too *tango*-ly.

What happened when the beetle had too much coffee?

It started dancing the jitterbug.

How do you clean a ballroom dance floor?

With a rhumba.

What do you call a folk dancer named Dorothy?

Polka Dot.

Knock knock.
Who's there?

Waltz.
Waltz who?

Waltz out here and dance with me.

TOE-TAPPING TICKLERS

How is *tap* dancing dangerous?

You could fall into the sink.

What did the exhausted dancer do?

He tapped out.

Why did the tap dancer trade a basketball for a football?

She was doing a ball change.

What's a tap dancer's favorite toy car?

A pullback.

How do tap dancers fight?

They get into a minor scuffle.

What do a tap dancer and an archeologist have in common?

They both use digs and brushes.

Why was the tap dancer hard to find?

He got lost in the shuffle.

How do you get a stubborn tap to dance?

I'm afraid you have to *faucet*!

What do you call a plumber who can also tap dance?

Multi-*fauceted*.

There was an issue with the ballroom floor last week.

It's okay. Everyone kept tap dancing around it.

Why do tap dancers make good computer hackers?

They can tap into the network.

What kind of dancing can you do on your back?

A spinal tap.

What is a tap dancer's favorite coffee drink?

A *tap*-puccino.

What is a tap dancer's favorite dessert?

Tap-ioca pudding.

Why did the embroiderer take up tap dancing?

To work on her *tap*-estry.

JAZZY JOKESTERS

How do jazz dancers cool off?

With a fan kick.

What do jazz dancers and astronauts have in common?

They can both do the moonwalk.

What does a jazz dancer order at a sushi restaurant?

One head roll, one shoulder roll, and several hip rolls.

What shape has four sides and good rhythm?

A jazz square.

How do dancers multiply a number by itself?

They jazz square it.

What is Captain Hook's best dance move?

A jazz hand.

What do you call a washed-up jazz dancer?

A *jazz*-been.

What is a jazz dancer's favorite fruit?

Jazz-berries.

How do you know when a dancer is guilty?

When they're caught *jazz*-handed!

Where does a cow learn how to Broadway dance?

Mooo-sical theater.

Why did Mr. Potato Head have to skip dance class?

He forgot to put on his jazz hands.

What kind of dance involves criminal deception?

Fraud-way!

How do jazz dancers get rid of a bad mood?

They finger snap out of it.

What do you call secret agents who can dance?

Jazzer-*spies*!

SECTION 6:
DANCING DELIGHTS

What move does a royal dancer do?

The King Charleston.

Why were the kids scared of the male dancer?

He was a boogie man.

Knock, knock.
Who's there?

Lettuce.
Lettuce who?

Lettuce dance all night!

Knock, knock.
Who's there.

Cory.
Cory who?

Choreography!

Knock, knock.
Who's there?

Ivana.
Ivana who?

Ivana dance with somebody!

Knock, knock.
Who's there?

May?
May who?

May I have this dance?

What was hiding in the dancer's closet?

The boogie monster.

Who teaches dance routines to flesh-eating zombies?

A *gore*-eographer.

Why did the dancer cross the road?

She had to do the combination on the other side.

How do hens dance?

Chick to chick.

How do you make a tissue dance?

Put a little boogie in it.

What kind of dance can you do on your stomach?

Belly dancing.

How many dancers does it take to screw in a light bulb?

Five–six–seven–eight!

Why did the dancer get rid of her root vegetables?

She couldn't keep a beet.

What is an avocado's favorite dance?

The *guac*-arena (gwok-uh-RAY-nah)!

What is a dentist's favorite dance?

The floss.

What's a horse's favorite dance?

The nae nae.

What song gets eggs grooving?

The Humpty Dance.

Where do fortune tellers dance?

At the crystal ball.

What kind of dance became popular because of a pandemic?

Social dis-*dancing*.

What kind of dance does Princess Leia do?

The resis-*dance*.

What do you get when the mafia performs a surprise public group dance?

Flash mobsters.

Why did the police officer pull over the U-Haul?

He was trying to bust a move.

What kind of dance is popular in Minecraft?

Square dancing.

What do ghosts dance to?

Soul music.

How can a salad make you dance?

When it has a good beet.

What kind of dance do you do when you don't like someone?

Avoi-*dance*.

How do clocks learn new dance moves?

By watching TikTok.

BARS AND RINGS AND OTHER SILLY THINGS

A gymnast walks into a bar.

"No, you're supposed to *swing around* it," said her coach.

Why are the uneven bars always looking for revenge?

They want to get even.

What gymnastics category is best for dogs?

The uneven barks!

How does a gymnast tell someone to slow down?

"Hold your pommel horses."

Why did Sister Maria win the gymnastics competition?

She was the best bar nun.

Why did the gymnast score low on the parallel bars?

He was unparalleled in every category.

Why could the gymnast never top his own personal best?

It was a high bar.

What did the coach say to the gymnasts who were goofing off?

"Stop your pommel-horsing around!"

What do gymnasts and lawyers have in common?

They both want to do well on the Bar.

What is a gymnast's favorite excuse?

"It's not my *vault*!"

Why were the gymnast's valuables extra safe?

He had a good vault.

I used to be afraid of the vault.

Then I got over it.

How do gymnasts check their balance?

At the bank.

Why was the gymnast in credit card debt?

His balance was outstanding.

The gymnast had a very symmetrical smile.

It was a balanced beam.

Why did the gymnast feel guilty?

Because she was at *vault*.

Who taught Mickey Mouse to do gymnastics?

Vault Disney.

What's a gymnast's favorite candy?

Chocolate *vault* balls.

HANDSTANDS, FLIPS, AND TUMBLING QUIPS

Why do gymnasts eat bland food in the winter?

They prefer summer-salt.

What happens when a gymnast has gas?

He does fartwheels.

What do you call an unfriendly gymnast?

Handstand-offish.

What are a gymnast's favorite chips?

Salto and vinegar.

Did you hear about the angry gymnast who made a dramatic exit?

She completely flipped out!

Which gymnast can flip higher than a building?

They all can. Buildings can't flip!

Why are gymnasts no good in emergencies?

They always flip out.

Why is it annoying to watch TV with a gymnast?

They're always channel-flipping.

Why should you surround yourself with gymnasts?

Because there's safety in tumblers.

Did you hear about the gymnast who fell in love mid-flip?

He was heels over head.

Why did the gymnast crash into the grocery store shelf?

There was something wrong with her shopping cartwheel.

What do you call a sandal that's bad at gymnastics?

A flip-flop.

I wanted to join a gymnastics class, but I had to bend over backward to get in.

What is the Little Mermaid's favorite gymnastics flip?

The aerial.

Did you hear about the gymnast who finally put his foot down?

He wouldn't handstand for it any longer.

How do you tell a gymnast to go away?

"Take a pike."

What is a rattlesnake's best gymnastics trick?

A diamond-back-handspring.

What is a gymnast's favorite season?

Hand Spring.

Why did the gymnast get a job at McDonalds?

To work on her double-double.

The audience applauded the gymnast's handstand.

It was the best, hands down.

Why did the gymnast become a crime fighter?

To take the law into her own handstand.

Why did the gymnast go to the thrift store?

To get a second-hand stand.

What's the best part about being a gymnast?

It's flippin' fun!

DISMOUNTS, SPLITS, AND GIGGLE FITS

The gymnast wasn't very flexible, so he bought some bananas.

Now he can do the splits.

48

Knock, knock.
Who's there?

Waiter.
Waiter who?

Waiter stick the landing!

Why did the gymnast bring a hammer to the competition?

She wanted to nail the dismount.

Why did the gymnast go on vacation to Mount Everest?

Her coach said, "DIS-mount n' have a rest."

What do you call a dismount that's a little off?

A discount.

What is a gymnast's favorite soup?

"Splits" pea!

The gymnast took a long break because of an injury.

But it's okay. She's getting back in the straddle again.

Knock, knock.

Who's there?

Dis Mountain.

Dis Mountain who?

Dismount n' try it again from the top.

How long does it take to write a gymnastics joke?

A "splits" second.

Why did the gymnast clear his schedule?

To be more flexible.

ACROBATIC ANTICS

What is a gymnast's favorite movie?

Lady and the Tramp-oline.

What do you call an acrobatic drummer?

A rhythmic gymnast.

Why do rhythmic gymnasts use ribbons?

To tie the routine together nicely.

What lives in a cave and can do gymnastics?

An acro-*bat*.

What do you call a gymnast duck?

A *quack*-robat.

What do you get when a gymnast plays baseball?

An acro-*batter*.

Where does Batman practice gymnastics?

His acro-*Batcave*.

What do you call a clumsy gymnast?

A stumbler.

What do you call a gymnast who's covered in glue?

Gymnasticky!

Why did the gymnast bring a broom to the Olympics?

To sweep away the competition.

What do you call a mean gymnast?

A gym-*nasty*.

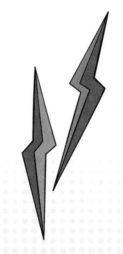

What do you call a bloodsucking parasite that does acrobatics?

A gymnas-*tick*.

Why is it tough to be a vegan gymnast?

Because of all the gymnastics *meets*.

Why did the gymnast buy a guillotine?

To improve her execution.

What did the ancient Egyptian queen wear to gymnastics class?

A *Cleo*-tard.

Why did the two gymnasts hate each other?

They were *arch*-enemies.

Knock, Knock.
Who's there?

2-4-6-8.
2-4-6-8 who—

–do we appreciate!

55

What did the cheerleader say when she did extra credit work?

Give me an A!

Why do plants make terrible cheerleaders?

They only root for themselves.

What did the cheerleader say when he walked into the coffee shop?

Give me a T!

How does a cheerleader sing Christmas carols?

"Fa-la-la-la-la-la, Rah-rah, rah, rah!"

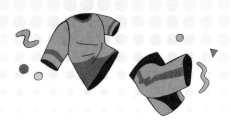

How do cheerleaders inflate a bike tire?

They *pump-pump-pump* it up!

What did the cheerleader say to her garden?

"Grow team, grow!"

What does a cheerleading sheep chant?

"Bah-bah-bah! We can't be bleat!"

What does a firefly cheerleader chant?

"Glow team, glow!"

Why did the cheerleader cheer when she saw her credit card statement?

She was told to root for the Bills.

How do cheerleaders get their kids up in the morning?

They cheer them up.

Why do cheerleaders make human pyramids?

Because spheres are pointless.

What is a cheerleader's favorite hot drink?

Liber-*tea*!

How do cheerleaders ride horses?

Side straddle.

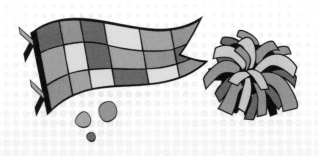

Why did the cheerleader need anger management classes?

She kept flipping out.

What did the Shakespearean cheerleader ask?

"Toe-touch or not toe-touch, that is the question."

Why did the cheerleaders throw the baby's crib in the air?

They were practicing a cradle catch.

What do cheerleaders and funk music have in common?

They both need a strong base.

What do you call a cheerleader who hasn't shaved?

Hairy Spotter.

Why was the cheerleader covered in yolks?

She put all her eggs in one basket toss.

Why did the cheerleader get a free airplane ticket?

She was a frequent flyer.

What is the zombie cheerleader's favorite stunt?

The deadman.

JOKES TO CHEER YOU UP

Why do ghosts make the best cheerleaders?

They're supernaturally spirited!

What do you call a cheerleader who's really annoyed?

Spirit-ated.

What's a cheerleader's favorite dog?

A *Pom-Pom*-eranian.

What do you call a group of invisible cheerleaders?

A sheer squad.

How do cheerleaders like their ice cream sundaes?

With a cheery on top.

Why do cheerleaders love the beach?

Because of all the *Pom-Pom* trees.

What happened when the cheerleader was questioned?

She skirted around the issue.

What's a cheerleader's favorite coffee drink?

Pom-Pom-kin spice latte.

What's a cheerleader's favorite fruit?

Pom-Pom-egranate.

What do you call a psychic cheerleader?

A *Pom-Pom* reader.

Why did the vampire attend the football game?

To get close to all the cheer *bleeders*.

What's a cheerleader's favorite soft drink?

It's a tie between *Root* beer and *Pep*-si

What happened to the cheerleader who killed the team mascot?

She got away *mascot* free!

Why were all the cheerleaders sneezing?

They were at a *pepper* rally.

What do cheerleaders eat for breakfast?

Cheery-o's.

Why can't cheerleaders watch horror movies?

They're too jumpy.

Why did the cheerleader eat the milky way?

To become an All-Star.

How do you describe a sleeping cheerleader?

Full of dream spirit.

TELLING FUNNY JOKES!

1. Know your joke.
Be sure you memorize the whole joke before you tell it. Most of us have heard someone start a joke by saying, "Oh, this is SO funny . . ." But then they can't remember part of it. Or they forget the ending, which is the most important part of the joke—the punch line!

2. Speak up.
Don't mumble your words. And don't speak too fast or too slow. Just speak clearly. You don't have to use a strange voice or accent. (Unless that's part of the joke!)

3. Look at your audience.
Good eye contact with your listeners will grab and hold their attention.

4. Don't overthink things.
You don't need to use silly gestures to tell your joke, unless it helps sell the punch line. You can either sit or stand to tell your jokes. Make yourself comfortable. Remember, telling jokes is basically just talking to people to make them laugh.

5. Don't laugh at your own joke.
Sure, comedians sometimes crack up laughing while they're telling a story. And that can be pretty funny by itself. But normally, it's best not to laugh at your own jokes. If you do, you might lose the timing of your joke or mess it up. Let your audience do the laughing. Your job is to be the funny one.

6. Practice your setup.

The setup is the second most important part of a joke. This includes everything you say before getting to the punch line. Be as clear as you can so when you reach the punch line, it makes sense!

7. Get the punch line right.

The punch line is the most important part of the joke. It's the payoff to the main event. A good joke is best if you pause for a second or two before delivering the punch line. That tiny pause will make your audience pay attention, eager to hear what's coming next.

8. Practice, practice, practice.

Practice your routine until you know it by heart. You can also watch other comedians or a comedy show or film. Listen to other people tell a joke. Pay attention to what makes them funny. You can pick up skills by seeing how others get an audience laughing. With enough practice, you'll soon be a great comedian.

9. It's all about the timing.

Learn to get the timing right for the biggest impact. Waiting for the right time and giving that extra pause before the punch line can really zing an audience. But you should also know when NOT to tell a joke. You probably know when your friends like to hear something funny. But when around unfamiliar people, you need to "read the room" first. Are people having a good time? Or is it a more serious event? A joke is funniest when it's told in the right setting.

DANCE, CHEER, AND GYMNASTICS TERMS TO KNOW

Ballet

arabesque (air-uh-BESK)—a ballet position in which the body is bent forward from the hip on one leg while one arm is extended forward and the other arm and leg stretch backward

fondu (fon-DOO)—a ballet move in which one lowers the body by bending the knee of the supporting leg

jeté (zhuh-TAY)—a ballet leap in which the dancer's weight is transferred from one foot to the other by "throwing" one leg to the front, side, or back, and then holding the other leg in any desired position upon landing

pas-de-bourreé (paw-duh-buh-RAY)—a walking or running ballet step usually done on the points of the toes in three small steps

pas-de-deux (paw-duh-DOO)—a two-person ballet dance, usually a duet for a man and a woman

passé (pah-SAY)—a ballet movement in which the foot of the working leg passes the knee of the supporting leg from one position to another

pirouette (PEER-ooh-ett)—a ballet move in which the dancer turns in place on one leg, with the raised foot touching the knee of the supporting leg

plié (plee-AY)—a movement in which a dancer bends the knees and straightens them again, usually with the feet turned out and heels firmly on the ground

pointe (POINT)—a ballet position in which the body is balanced on the extreme tips of the toe in specially designed shoes

tendu (tahn-DOO)—a basic ballet move in which the working leg is extended along the floor until only the tip of the toe remains touching the floor

Ballroom/Salsa

bachata (bah-CHAH-tah)—a style of dance from the Dominican Republic connected with popular Latin American music

cha-cha (CHAH-chah)—a lively Latin dance characterized by three quick steps followed by two slower beats

flamenco (flah-MENG-koh)—a solo dance characterized by hand clapping, stamping feet, and intricate hand, arm, and body movements

merengé (mer-ENG-ay)—a ballroom dance in which one foot is dragged on every step

rhumba (ROOM-bah)—a ballroom dance that uses a basic step-close-step pattern and pronounced hip movements

tango (TANG-goh)—a ballroom dance characterized by marked rhythms and postures and abrupt pauses

waltz (WALTZ)—a ballroom dance performed by a couple, who as a pair turn together as they progress around the dance floor

Tap

brush (BRUSH)—a tap step where the ball of your foot strikes the ground while brushing forward

dig (DIG)—a tap step in which you dig the heel of one foot into the floor without weight transfer

pullback (PULL-bak)—a tap step done by hopping on one foot with a back brush in the air, and then landing on the same foot

scuffle (SKUF-uhl)—a tap step in which the heel of the foot hits the ground with forward movement, followed by a backward brush of the ball of the foot

shuffle (SHUF-uhl)—a tap step in which the ball of the foot strikes the ground while brushing forward, followed by a backward brush of the ball of the foot

Miscellaneous Dance

floss (FLAHSS)—a popular dance move in which a person repeatedly swings their arms, with clenched fists, from the back of their body to the front, on each side

Macarena (MACK-uh-RAY-nuh)—a dance done to the Spanish song "Macarena"

nae nae (NAY nay)—a dance move in which one raises their hand and swerves it left and right while the other hand is on the hip

Cheerleading and Gymnastics

aerial (AIR-ee-uhl)—a move in which a gymnast completes a full rotation in the air without touching the apparatus with the hands

back handspring (BAK HAND-spring)—a move in which a gymnast takes off from one or two feet, jumps backward onto the hands, and pushes off to land on the feet; also known as a "flic-flac" or "flip-flop"

base (BAYS)—stunt position that does the lifting

basket toss (BAS-ket TOSS)—stunt where bases throw the flyer into the air and the flyer performs a skill before being caught; the bases' hands interlock like a woven basket

deadman (DED-man)—a stunt where the flyer falls backward or forward out of a stunt and is caught by several bases

liberty (LIB-ur-tee)—a cheer move in which the toe of the non-standing leg is raised to the standing knee, with both knees facing forward

pike (PIKE)—a position in which legs are kept straight and brought close to the upper body, so the lower and upper body form an L-shape

pom-pom (PAHM-pahm)—a cheer prop made of shreds of colorful plastic used to emphasize motions and grab the audience's attention

salto (SAL-toh)—a flip or somersault where a gymnast rotates around the axis of the hips

ABOUT THE AUTHOR

Megan Woodward grew up traveling all over the world, but always felt at home with her head in a book and watching old movies. Combining her love of the written word with her love of film, she got an MFA in screenwriting from UCLA. Her debut picture book, *This Book is Definitely NOT Cursed*, will be released in 2024 by Simon and Schuster.

Megan loves all things funny, from puns to satire and sarcasm to slapstick. When she's not busy writing, she can be found cooking, dancing, laughing, singing, reading, or all five at once. Which is a great way to either embarrass her kid or almost burn down the house. She lives in Portland, Oregon, where it rains entirely too much, but never on her parade.

READ THEM ALL!

JAKE MADDOX SPORTS JOKES

GUT-BUSTING
BASKETBALL
JOKES AND PUNS

JAKE MADDOX SPORTS JOKES

HILARIOUS
DANCE, CHEER, AND GYMNASTICS
JOKES AND PUNS

JAKE MADDOX SPORTS JOKES

LAUGH-OUT-LOUD
FOOTBALL
JOKES AND PUNS

JAKE MADDOX SPORTS JOKES

SIDE-SPLITTING
SOCCER
JOKES AND PUNS